Walther Ziegler

AF187038

Adorno
in 60 Minutes

Translated by
Alexander Reynolds

My thanks go to Rudolf Aichner for his tireless critical editing; Silke Ruthenberg for the fine graphics; Lydia Pointvogl, Eva Amberger, Christiane Hüttner, and Dr. Martin Engler for their excellent work as manuscript readers and sub-editors; Prof. Guntram Knapp, who first inspired me with enthusiasm for philosophy; and Angela Schumitz, who handled in the most professional manner, as chief editorial reader, the production of both the German and the English editions of this series of books.

My special thanks go to my translator

Dr Alexander Reynolds.

Himself a philosopher, he not only translated the original German text into English with great care and precision but also, in passages where this was required in order to ensure clear understanding, supplemented this text with certain formulations adapted specifically to the needs of English-language readers.

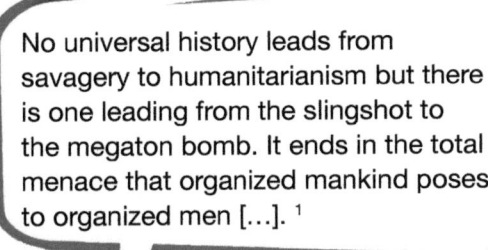

No universal history leads from savagery to humanitarianism but there is one leading from the slingshot to the megaton bomb. It ends in the total menace that organized mankind poses to organized men [...]. [1]

Bibliographic Information held by the German National Library: The details of the original German edition of this publication are held by the German National Library as part of the German National Bibliography; detailed bibliographical data can be found online at www.dnb.de.

© 2020 Dr Walther Ziegler
1st Edition March 2020
Jacket design and graphic design for the whole book: Silke Ruthenberg, making use of illustrations by:
Raphael Bräsecke, Creactive – Studio for Advertising, Comics & Illustrations
© JackF - Fotolia.com (image-frames)
© Valerie Potapova - Fotolia.com (image-frames)
© Svetlana Gryankina - Fotolia.com (speech-balloons)

Publisher and Printing:
BoD – Books on Demand, Norderstedt
ISBN 978-3-7504-6023-2

Inhalt

Adorno's Great Discovery

Theodor W. Adorno (1903-1969) counts still today as one of the most charismatic and intellectually imposing thinkers in the whole history of philosophy. Already during his lifetime he exerted great influence on the student movements that so deeply marked the post-war German Federal Republic and indeed on the intellectual climate of this young republic in general. No other German intellectual of the period between 1959 and 1969 lectured so frequently on public radio and TV channels as did Adorno.

As did Sartre in France, Adorno became, in Germany, a charismatic point of orientation for student protestors and indeed for the New Left as a whole. He also resembled Sartre in other respects: both men were small and stocky, wore horn-rimmed glasses to correct their overstrained sight, and were known to have conducted many affairs with attractive women. His lectures, that many students from other parts of Europe and even from America travelled thousands of miles to attend, were always packed – though very few of those who attended them could honestly

7

claim to have understood all that they heard there. The immensely complex lines of reasoning spun out at the lectern by the little bald man in horn-rimmed glasses, and such strenuously abstract books of his as the late masterpiece *Negative Dialectics*, are still looked on today in Germany as intellectual hurdles that only the greatest intellectual athletes can hope to clear.

His work contains, among other things, a rigorous critique of the capitalist system, so that he is often considered to have prepared the ground for the great wave of social protest that shook many countries in 1968. There is certainly some truth to this, even if he was dismayed by many aspects of this great revolt that broke out, also at his own German university, in the year before his death and refused, to the disappointment of some of his admirers, to play the role of a leader of this movement.

Adorno's central idea is a paradoxical and provocative one. Modern capitalist society has gone entirely and fundamentally astray. Individuals in this society enjoy, indeed, unprecedented advantages in terms of mobility, technology, medical care and other forms of prosperity; but at the same time we have lost, collectively, all that makes life really worth living, namely: a sense for Nature (including, perhaps most importantly, for the natural beings that we ourselves are) and, in the end, even the ability to love:

> Every person today, without exception, feels too little loved because every person cannot love enough.[2]

This, modern Man's loss of the ability to love is, Adorno believes, a direct consequence of the commodity and consumer society. Human beings become calculating and calculable because in a society based solely on "exchange value" everything and everyone has a fixed and determined price. Every commodity, and first and foremost the commodity that is an individual's labour-power, is and has to be carried to market and sold. This leads, in the end, to human actions and relations appearing to those involved in them as external, exchangeable "things" that they themselves, as humans, have no real part in. In a society where nothing is ever done unless it is paid for, the once-natural concern for the fate of others gradually vanishes. Everyone fights for their own advantage alone. "Me Incorporated" becomes a symbol of our modern world.

What's more, Adorno is not criticizing here just the fact that in market societies like ours everything is appraised in terms of supply and demand; he is also pointing out that consumer societies make it their job to awaken ever new artificial "needs" in the consumer, so that commodities become, in these societies, fetishes that enjoy an almost religious veneration.

For many people in today's society, for example, a car is much more than just a means of getting around. They invest their own identity in this lifeless object to such an extent that they derive their whole sense of their value as human beings from the make and quality of car they own. Capitalism turns individuals into dependent beings, penetrating and deforming their whole character. Adorno believed so strongly in this notion of our having been wholly and entirely distorted by the world we have created that he included in his most personal work, the *Minima Moralia*, a pithy little thesis that turned completely on its head the famous thesis of a philosopher, Hegel, whom he greatly admired but who had taken, in the end, a positive and even apologetic stance toward the modern world around him. "The truth is the whole", Hegel had concluded in the 1820s; just over a hundred years later, Adorno's conclusion was:

The whole is the false.[3]

This general suspicion cast upon modern capitalist society in its entirety earned Adorno the reputation of being the most significant of the various representatives of what is called "Critical Theory", a body of thought which did indeed set itself the task of analysing and critiquing capitalist society not just, as Marx and the early Marxists had, in its economic basis but in all its social and cultural ramifications. Since all the thinkers associated with this current in social philosophy had been associated, in the 1920s and 30s, as teachers or researchers with the Institute for Social Research of the University of Frankfurt, "Critical Theory" is also sometimes referred to as "the Frankfurt School".

The "Frankfurt School" thinkers included, besides Adorno, such writers famous in their own right as Max Horkheimer, Herbert Marcuse and the psychoanalyst Erich Fromm. These philosophers all sharply criticized the ossified structures of post-war capitalist societies. In practicing this critique they still made frequent reference to Marx and continued to describe themselves as philosophical "materialists".

But in the face of the degeneration of Soviet Marxism into Stalinism and of the transformation, in the West, of the "proletarian" more and more into a "consumer", the Critical Theorists came to consider world communist revolution as a less and less realistic prospect. They replaced Marx's notions of the inevitability of the worldwide overthrow of the existing order and the imminent realization of a classless society with the notion of the need for a permanent critique of existing society. Hence the name "Critical Theory".

It was in exile from his German homeland that Adorno authored, together with Max Horkheimer, his friend since their student days, the book that counts as the primary work of Critical Theory: *The Dialectic of Enlightenment*. The two men, like the other prominent Critical Theorists Fromm and Marcuse, had had to flee to the USA, due to their Jewish origins, when Hitler seized power in 1933. *The Dialectic of Enlightenment*, written in the country that gave them refuge, counts still today as one of the most important standard works of sociology and social philosophy.

The book represented a watershed in social philosophy because it was the first to develop a "critique of critique". "Enlightenment", embodied in the works of such great early-modern thinkers as Rousseau, Voltaire, Diderot, Kant, Hume and Locke, had been, itself, a great enterprise of social critique.

These 17th and 18th century "Enlighteners" critiqued feudalism, the divine right of kings, religion and all superstition and aspired to free human beings once and for all from all the old irrational constraints passed down from the Middle Ages. "Who should rule the people if not the people themselves?" ran one of their progressive rallying cries. The Enlightenment, in other words, was the great age of critical thinking.

Adorno and Horkheimer returned from their American exile, however, bearing with them a great suspicion of this generally accepted truth. The whole critically emancipatory movement that was the early modern Enlightenment signified for Europe, they now argued, not just the welcome opening of a new era but also a sort of calamity. It too, then, needed to be subjected to a rigorous critique. The Enlightenment era, indeed, had seen much progress in political, intellectual and technical fields; but all these improvements had had a troubling "flip side" to them.

Already the opening sentence of the first chapter of *The Dialectic of Enlightenment* sums up the problem:

> Enlightenment, understood in the widest sense as the advance of thought, has always aimed at liberating human beings from fear and installing them as masters. Yet the wholly enlightened earth is radiant with triumphant calamity.[4]

The Enlightenment, so ran Adorno's argument here, had originally pursued the progressive aim of relieving human beings of the fears that had tormented them through so many dark centuries: fear of Nature, of wild animals and of failed harvests, as well as irrational, superstitious fears such as that of the Last Judgment, the Apocalypse or the Devil. The Enlightenment did indeed aspire to let the light of science and reason shine on and illuminate every area of human life, driving out and replacing that irrational belief whereby our destinies are determined by imponderable higher powers.

Enlightenment marks the end of the thousands of years in which peasants gazed fearfully up at the sky and made sacrifices to the thunder-god to dissuade him from ruining their crops with hail or heavy rain and the beginning of an era in which storm-clouds are scientifically dispersed by the release of chemicals from aeroplanes. In our enlightened age Nature is no longer experienced as all-powerful and threatening. Rather, our modern combine-harvesters, pesticides, fungicides and factory-farming methods have made of it something that we completely dominate and control. And yet today, in the phrase of Adorno's already quoted, "the wholly enlightened earth is radiant with triumphant calamity". Because total control over Nature has its price:

Human beings purchase the increase in their power with estrangement from that over which it is exerted.[5]

The more perfectly human beings succeed in controlling the world and our own coexistence by means of hyper-modern machinery and sophisticated social institutions the farther we remove ourselves not only from external Nature but also from that Nature which constitutes our own most intimate inner being. Adorno gives a grave diagnosis, perhaps the gravest diagnosis possible, of our modern civilization. We may indeed, through the unleashed power of science and an omnipresent social administration, have raised ourselves to the position of lords over Nature. But in doing so we have enslaved ourselves. We have become the manipulated victims of the mass society that we ourselves created.

Our lives consist in phantasms and illusions. We still, indeed, have a subjective sense that our day-to-day experience is a real one. We think we live in a real world with all its problems, worries and bright spots of hope and joy; but in reality we find ourselves in a mere appearance of life or, as Adorno calls it, an "entangling web of artificial blindness". This extends so far, Adorno argues, that what appear to be "people" are often just irrelevant epiphenomena on the surface of what is in fact a person-less mass:

In many people it is already an impertinence to say 'I'.[6]

We become, in a phrase coined by Adorno's colleague Marcuse, examples of "one-dimensional Man", incapable of desiring anything except that which the consumption-goods industry trains us to desire by dangling it before our eyes.

This suspicion that we might be victims of a total manipulation is not a new one. It is as old, indeed, as Plato who, already two and a half millennia before Adorno, imagined, with his famous "allegory of the cave", the manipulation of men chained up in a cavern into no longer recognizing the real world outside as the real world and into taking for reality what were in fact just shadows flickering on the cavern wall.

Adorno, however, goes a step further than Plato. Whereas Plato's "allegory of the cave" still allows the imagined human prisoners the chance of climbing up toward the light and attaining the real world, in Adorno's vision the imprisoned are damned to remain imprisoned forever. Plato urges us to keep our inner eye fixed on the truth, believing that this alone will enable us to lead a good and authentic life. But Adorno's assessment of the present human condition is much more pessimistic. We have by now all become too firmly lodged into the mechanism of the capitalist world, as its living working parts, for us to manage to leave "the cave" at all:

There is no longer any position outside of the mechanism that might be taken up, no position from which we might name that which haunts our haunted world.[7]

And even if we feel that something is not as it should be with our life, that something has gone seriously wrong with the world, we are hardly in a position to correct it, since:

Wrong life cannot be lived rightly.[8]

This dark, pithy phrase of Adorno's is famous in the German-speaking world and often cited. Even eighty years after being set to paper it still sums up the sense of uncertainty and inescapable self-contradiction that plagues modern Man. On the one hand we citizens of Western civilization enjoy, to a degree that no one ever has before, the blessings of the technical and medical innovations, as well as all the more frivolous benefits in the way of consumer goods and media spectacles, that characterize modern capitalist society; on the other hand, however, we have a sense that we are losing ourselves in these new structures and stimulations and are becoming slaves not just to our real material needs but also to many false needs that this modern capitalist society creates and implants in us. We experience a deep longing for some life more "real" than the flood of distracting stimuli that fills and forms every minute of our day; but somehow we never manage to actually live this "real life" that we long for, because we feel ourselves, by now, much too comfortably at home in the false one. Many people today, for example, would find it completely impossible to live without a TV set, which evening after evening carries into their living room a pseudo-world which is compellingly entertaining – but at the same time utterly unreal.

Even Adorno's critics concede that his critique of post-war consumer society puts its finger on many valid truths and that much of what he says applies as well, or even better, to the society of our twenty-first century than it did to that of the twentieth. Is the life we lead really a "false life"? Are all our thoughts and actions directed by powers that we cannot really call our own? And if so, how can Adorno know that it is so? Has the project of the Enlightenment, namely, that of freeing Man from superstition through reason and science, really ended up achieving the opposite aim from the one it set itself? Is Critical Theory right? Does science and its rational calculations give rise, in the end, to the danger of a new barbarism? Adorno's answers to these questions are always highly original and always fascinating.

Adorno's Central Idea

The Dialectic of Enlightenment

The decisive catalyst for the forming of Adorno's central idea was surely the experience of German Fascism and the Holocaust that it committed. On his return, then, from his American exile to a Germany almost totally destroyed by the war, it was two key questions, above all, that preoccupied Adorno. The first and most important of all was: how can we prevent Fascism, and most particularly such fruits of Fascism as the Nazi extermination camp at Auschwitz, from ever occurring again?

> The premier demand upon all education is that Auschwitz not happen again. Its priority before any other requirement is such that I believe I need not and should not justify it.[9]

The second question was a more retrospective and analytical one, though to answer it was certainly to go some way toward answering the first: how was it even possible that, after hundreds of years of European humanism and Enlightenment, barbaric totalitarian rulers and regimes should have come to power, in the middle of the twentieth century, in no less than three great European countries: Spain, Italy and Germany?

Already during his exile Adorno had carried out social-psychological research related to this question and he continued these researches once back in Germany. The results, which were published in 1950 under the title *The Authoritarian Personality*, were shocking. Adorno's evaluation of the various interviews conducted for the study concluded that, even after the experience of Nazism, some two thirds of the German population still took a sceptical attitude to the notion of a democratic political system. Half of the Germans interviewed rejected the idea that they and their countrymen bore any share of guilt for the terrible actions of the Nazi regime.

And a large proportion of them gave answers which were at least indirect indications that their personality-structures were such that they would willingly submit to some new authoritarian "strong man", were one to emerge. But for Adorno these empirical findings were not the decisive thing. They revealed only facts which he had in any case already suspected to be the case. His great philosophical question was rather the following: how was it possible, after all the sterling service to the cause of the Enlightenment that is to be found in the work of men like Rousseau, Voltaire, Montesquieu, Leibniz, Kant, and Locke, for Europe and its population to still remain so susceptible to lapsing back into the darkness of brutal barbarism?

The answer that he offered to this question became the point of departure for the whole of Critical Theory. Enlightenment and modern science, argued Adorno, have indeed freed human beings from superstition. But they have established in its place a purely instrumental explanation of the world which is really no less dangerous. Because this strictly technocratic, instrumental account of the world and its meaning is one which runs a serious risk of leading back into the very irrationalism that it was meant to liberate from.

The cause of the problem here is that the concern animating science and scientific investigation has tended, from the start, to be that of how whatever is investigated and scientifically understood can be put to use:

> Enlightenment stands in the same relation to things as the dictator to human beings. He knows them to the extent that he can manipulate them. The man of science knows things to the extent that he can make them.[10]

"Find out what can be done with it" is the overriding imperative of modern science. Scientists, Adorno points out, do not wish just to rationally analyse and understand the world and the things that make it up but want in every case also to control these things. With every new bit of knowledge that is acquired one further step is taken in the moulding, dominating and manipulating of Nature. This is why science, in its very essence, has, as Adorno puts it, something "dictatorial" about it.

Darwin's scientific development of a theory of evolution, for example, was originally very much an act of liberation: namely, from the irrational biblical myth of Man's creation, overnight, directly by the hand of God. Very soon, however, a highly irrational use and applicability was found for this eminently rational discovery of Darwin's. With his hypothesis of a process of "natural selection" in the animal kingdom Darwin had in fact, probably unintentionally, created a seedbed for the much more sinister hypothesis that such a principle of selection also governed human evolution.

Already half a century before Hitler the British scientist and philosopher Herbert Spencer took the doctrine of "natural selection" and applied it to the sphere of human society and history, founding what came to be known as "Social Darwinism". He coined the phrase "survival of the fittest" and declared the struggle between peoples, races and nations to be a natural process. Darwin's "natural selection" was suddenly no longer just a description of the interaction of certain natural forces; it was now made exploitable in terms of a specific human agenda, in this case a targeted agenda of "race war". It was this agenda that was eagerly pursued a few decades later by the hundreds of real or purported scholars, professors, doctors and geneticists who were appointed, under Hitler's Nazi regime, to newly founded university chairs in "Racial Science". These supposed "scientists" spent their time gathering anatomical data on members of various ethnic groups, ranging from skull dimensions and physiognomies to height, skin pigmentation and IQ. Where this ended we already know.

With the rise of the "race delusion", then, we observe an initially rational science turning into an irrationalism contemptuous of human beings. In the wake of Darwin's originally rationally-grounded hypothesis regarding the origin of species and their development through natural selection there gradually grew up, under the covering mantle of science, the irrational myth of an "Aryan race" whose superior genetics would ensure their dominance over all the rest of the world:

(Thus) with every step Enlightenment entangles itself more deeply in mythology.[11]

To illustrate this inherent tendency of Enlightenment to turn back into the mythical superstition that it originally set out to overcome Adorno uses the anthropological concept of the "horde". Such "hordes" had existed already in the properly speaking "mythological" era of humanity, the Stone Age, when the individual members of a mass of hunters or gatherers felt themselves bound together as if into a single body by the common belief in some mythical story or symbol – for example, the whole "horde"'s identification with a single "spirit animal".

In the modern era, Adorno notes, such "hordes" make their appearance again. But this time what binds them together are purportedly rational explanations provided in the name of science: e.g. that certain masses of people "belong together" by reason of their all stemming from some single genetically identical sub-species or some "community of the race". Such "scientific" arguments were, and continue to be, advanced even where the differences between one supposed "race" and another prove to be minimal.

Those individuals too, then, who buy into this notion of a modern "horde" in the form of a racially defined "national community" are succumbing, centuries after the supposed age of Enlightenment, to the superstition that the Enlightenment felt it had put an end to. Only this time it is a "scientific" superstition. This is, however, Adorno further argues, not just a matter of a lapse back into barbarism but rather displays a quality of its own which must be sought in the logic of the Enlightenment itself:

> The "horde", a term which doubtless is to be found in the Hitler Youth organization, is not a relapse into the old barbarism but the triumph of repressive *égalité*, the degeneration of the equality of rights into the wrong inflicted by equals.[12]

The good intentions of the movement of Enlightenment, in this case those behind the call for the equality of all human beings, are interpreted here by Adorno as also, unintendedly, paving the way for totalitarianism. He points out that these good intentions could easily, much like the results of the university chairs in "Racial Science", be misused as bases for the reduction of all citizens to compliant members of a single "fraternity of shared blood". Because, under such circumstances, anyone who dared to criticize the regime was taken thereby to have quit the genetically-defined egalitarian "horde" and to have automatically become an "enemy of the people": someone who wanted to place himself outside of, or even above, the fraternal, equal "community of the nation".

The movement we call Enlightenment began as a critique of the power of Nature over Man and specifically of the notion that certain social institutions were so rooted in Nature that they could not be opposed or altered. It aspired to replace this power of Nature, and of the "second Nature" of supposedly eternal social institutions, with the critical power of Reason. But in the end it succeeded only in replacing those constraints of Nature and "second Nature" expressed through the taboos of myth and religion with equally constraining taboos in the form of pseudo-science and its instrumentalizing rationality:

Any attempt to break the compulsion of Nature by breaking Nature only succumbs more deeply to that compulsion. That has been the trajectory of European civilization.[13]

Even after the period of Fascism and the Second World War science and technology have still proven unable to free the human race in any real sense but have rather bound us into ever new forms of machinery. The institution of capitalism itself, Adorno points out, has now come to be perceived by many as eternally, immovably rooted in Nature, much like the social institutions that Enlightenment had most vigorously criticized, such as the divine right of kings or the "natural" inequality of the different classes of men. Many scientists look on egoism and the single-minded pursuit of personal profit as absolutely necessary natural drives, without which there would be no spirit of invention, no economic growth and no opening-up of new resources.

Best-selling books like *The Selfish Gene* by the respected scientist Richard Dawkins suggest that the "possessive individualism" which characterizes more and more cultures around the world is firmly rooted in unalterable natural fact.

On top of this comes the problem of "the technological veil". Since, with every passing year, technology is pervading our world more deeply and thoroughly, a thicker and thicker veil is coming to cover its original function as a mere tool to achieve ends chosen by human beings. Technology is acquiring a life of its own.

People are inclined to take technology to be the thing itself, as an end in itself, a force of its own, and they forget that it is an extension of human dexterity.[14]

What were once just technical means to ends have now become "fetishized", often tempting their users into fantasies of megalomania:

And which driver is not tempted, merely by the power of his engine, to wipe out the vermin of the street: pedestrians, children, cyclists?[15]

The movement of Enlightenment, then, so Adorno concludes, and all the technological development that went along with it have ended up becoming the very opposite of what they set out to be. Instead of liberating the human race, they have brought us into new and threatening structures of dependence.

Self-Repression Through Reason: The Example of Odysseus

Adorno offers as a concrete example of this dialectical reversal the story told of the experiences of the Ancient Greek hero Odysseus. This legendary hero embodies in his own person, argues Adorno, the dialectic of Enlightenment. Odysseus stands out from the other heroes featured in Homer's account of the Trojan War and its aftermath in relying not just on strength and martial valour but also, to a great degree, on reason and intelligence. For this reason, Odysseus represents, within the mythical world of antiquity, the earliest personification of the rational type of human being typical of our modernity. He is, as Adorno puts it

[...] the prototype of the bourgeois individual [...].[16]

The success that Odysseus achieves he achieves above all thanks to rational calculation and to an iron self-discipline and self-control. It is by a clever and disciplined trick, for example, that he succeeds in doing what no one had ever done: hearing the seductive, but fatal, song of the Sirens and living to tell the tale. Many ships, as the myth goes, had been drawn into shipwreck by the Sirens' entrancing song. Odysseus, however, orders his crew to put wax in their ears as they row past the Sirens' island and has them tie him, their captain, to the mast so that – although he can hear the song – he is powerless to do what many others have done and throw himself on the rocks to hear it better. Odysseus does what no one has ever done, then, and survives. But he does this only at the cost of having himself put in chains: a mythical image that Adorno interprets as an allegory of the modern subject's denying his own natural desires.

Adorno sees the same modern self-denial expressed in still more symbolical terms in another key episode of Homer's "Odyssey": the encounter with the Cyclops Polyphemus. Held captive by Polyphemus, Odysseus succeeds in escaping only through a literal self-denial. On being asked his name by the monstrous one-eyed Cyclops Odysseus had cunningly replied "Nobody". So that, when Odysseus and his men have put out the Cyclops's one eye and this latter is reduced to appealing to his fellow monsters to prevent his prisoners' escape, he can only cry out "Nobody has blinded me! Look for nobody!" – an appeal which leaves his fellow Cyclops puzzled and causes them to return to their own caves, thinking there is nothing wrong. Odysseus survives here too, then. But here too he does so only at the price of self-denial.

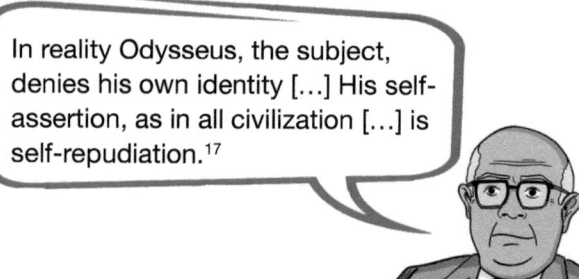

In reality Odysseus, the subject, denies his own identity [...] His self-assertion, as in all civilization [...] is self-repudiation.[17]

Just this, Adorno contends, is the inevitable fate of modern Man. Survival in mass society demands of us adaptation, self-repression and self-denial. Odysseus lived through all of this before us, back at the very dawn of civilization:

The nimble-witted man survives only at the cost of his own dream [...] by disintegrating his own magic [...]

He [...] must always be able to wait, to be patient, to renounce; he may not eat of the lotus or of the cattle of Hyperion.[18]

"With the *Odyssey*, then", so argue the authors of *The Dialectic of Enlightenment*, Homer composed nothing less than "the basic text of European civilization"[19]. His legendary figure of Odysseus anticipates the new human type that was going to dominate all the subsequent centuries of human history:

The lone voyager armed with cunning is already *homo oeconomicus*, whom all reasonable people will one day resemble.[20]

The Philosophy of the Marquis de Sade as a Consequence of Enlightenment

Adorno and Horkheimer find further indication of the truth of their basic thesis that Enlightenment runs a risk of turning into its opposite in the philosophy propounded by the Marquis de Sade, who was certainly a "man of the Enlightenment" at least in the sense that he lived most of his life, which ran from 1740 to 1814, in the 18th century, called the *siècle des Lumières*.

De Sade is known to most people only because of his perverse sexual practices. He was, however, besides being the man who gave his name to "sadism", also the author of numerous books and a prominent representative, along with La Mettrie and D'Holbach, of French philosophical materialism. This philosophical movement looked on itself as the spearhead of the 18th-century Enlightenment. In the years before and during the French Revolution these men critiqued religion as mere superstition and proposed a vision of the world that was strictly materialistic, natural-scientific and even, as some of them put it, "mechanical".

Human beings are in reality, so ran the argument of

these French philosophical materialists, not creatures of God, nor are they beings of pure spirit guided by abstract moral laws. Rather, they are living, material beings guided by the physical laws of Nature and to understand human beings one has to investigate these laws.

Thus La Mettrie for example, in his highly successful book *L'Homme Machine*, gave an account of the human being as a "man-machine", a kind of perfectly functioning piece of clockwork. "The human body," wrote La Mettrie, "is a machine that winds up its own springs" [21].

The other man of the Enlightenment D'Holbach, who wrote over four hundred articles on the natural sciences for Diderot's great *Encyclopaedia*, considered the sole cause of action in human beings to be our natural drives: "Man is a being purely physical [...] His visible actions are [...] the natural effects of his peculiar mechanism [...] All that he does, all that he is, is nothing more than what universal Nature has made him." [22]

As regards morality and moral philosophy, these French philosophical materialists defended the view that what human beings ought to do was simply follow the promptings of their natural drives, i.e. of their self-interest. The time, they argued, had come to recognize once again those claims of Nature which had, for thousands of years, been repressed and denied in the name of "God" or of "the higher, spiritual principle in Man". What is "moral", it should henceforth be accepted, is simply what is natural, what Nature prompts us to do.

The most radical of all these French philosophical materialists of the 18th century was the Marquis de Sade. He too understood himself to form the "spearhead" of Enlightenment but he was still more ruthlessly consistent than even thinkers like La Mettrie and D'Holbach in tracing out the logical consequences of the notion of "a life in conformity with Nature". If we acknowledge, argued de Sade, that we are simply and entirely natural beings whose actions unfold from our inner drives as the hands of a clock from its inner clockwork, then we are bound also to recognize our innate aggressiveness as a natural and acceptable thing, and this right up to the point of the pleasure we take in murder. In one of his main works, *Juliette, or Vice Amply Rewarded*, de Sade even describes murder as a necessary component part of Nature: "And where does this impetuous inclination come from? From Nature. Murder is one of its laws. Whenever Nature feels the need to murder it inspires us with the inclination to do so and we obey whether we wish to or not." [23]

De Sade's line of argument is simple. If everything human is, in the last analysis, a matter of natural predisposition and if Nature, in its turn, is something that science proves to be completely value-neutral, then one cannot consistently pass a negative value-judgment on murder, since this too is merely an event in Nature. De Sade has his heroine in this novel appear first in the role of an enthusiastic "Enlightener", critiquing the Catholicism in which she has been raised on the grounds that scientific proof for it is lacking:

(Juliette) demonizes Catholicism as the latest mythology, and with it civilization as a whole. [24]

He then, however, has her engage in a whole series of criminal experiences, including even committing several murders, until she finally, stripped of all illusions, comes to the conclusion that the exercise of violence is always a part of every human life. The condition, then, of a truly enlightened, free, and self-determined life consists not in renunciation, humility and a "love of one's fellow man" for which there is no scientific foundation but rather in a Nature-based "right to everything", not excluding the use of violence and even murder. Adorno and Horkheimer see in this argument of Juliette's a dangerous modern scientific attitude which is oriented exclusively to such natural elements, determinable by the positive sciences, as instincts, drives and really quantifiable crimes, and which accepts these latter too as growing spontaneously out of our nature:

Juliette's credo is science [...] She manipulates semantics and logical syntax like the most up-to-date positivist [...] as a daughter of the militant Enlightenment.[25]

In the midst of the French Revolution de Sade issued an appeal to his fellow Frenchmen to "make one more effort if you want truly to become republicans!"[26] This was the title of a sort of libertine manifesto read

out, in the midst of an orgy, by one of the protago-
nists of his 1795 novel *Philosophy in the Boudoir*. In it,
those already engaged in the project of revolutionary
republicanism are encouraged to carry the Enlightenment's demand for individual liberty through to
its logical conclusion; having already dispossessed
the clergy and beheaded the king, it argues, they
should take the final step of declaring themselves
in favour of the absolute freedom of the individual.
This means, for de Sade, a declaration that one is in
favour of the absolute freedom to commit any crime.
With ruthless logical consistency de Sade demands
the founding of a completely libertine state and an
attitude of "enlightened" tolerance vis-à-vis such as-
sociations devoted to uninhibited indulgence of the
instincts as an imagined "Society of the Friends of
Crime".[27]

Adorno and Horkheimer consider this, de Sade's radical demand for a "freedom to commit any crime", to
be evidence supporting their thesis that the Enlightenment, despite its beginning as a rational movement to liberate Man from religion, can always, due
to its materialism and rationalism, end up turning
into its opposite, i.e. into a complete unfreedom and
even into a threat to human life arising from the jus-
tification of violence as a natural human drive:

[…] The work of de Sade, like that of Nietzsche […] pushes the scientific principle to annihilating extremes.[28]

The Co-Optation of the Individual by the Culture Industry

The dialectic of Enlightenment becomes especially recognizable if one takes a closer look at the modern entertainment industry and at mass cultural production in general, to which Adorno refers by the general term "culture industry". One of the ways in which Enlightenment had originally set out to free people was that of cultivating them into creative and imaginative individuals. Insofar, however, as the world the Enlightenment produced is one of mass media, the people that have actually been created tend to be passive consumers who seek from culture only instantaneous pleasure. The original task assigned to art, which was that of touching people's emotions and prompting them to reflect on their situations, has been lost almost without trace. The art of narrative, for example, survives in our fully "enlightened" world only as variants on the same "stock plots", mechanically injected with maximum amounts of "fun factor", rolling off the same production line. Modern Man is bombarded with "light entertainment" as intensely and as ceaselessly as the soldiers in the trenches of the First World War were bombarded with shells and gunfire:

Fun is a medicinal bath that the entertainment industry never ceases to prescribe. It makes laughter the instrument for cheating happiness.[29]

In this way, an art that had once been defined by each work's unique individuality degenerates into a mass product, such as the productions of "the cinematic arts" in our present day whose quality tends to be measured solely in terms of the number of tickets sold at the box office. The script that swims, as regards its theme or the way the scriptwriter handles it, against the tide that forms the "mainstream" has little or no chance of ever actually being made into a film:

In film, any manuscript which is not reassuringly based on a bestseller is viewed with mistrust.[30]

The goal, then, of capitalist media- and art-production is to achieve the maximum profit possible. But at the same time the system trains, as it were, the taste of those who live under modern capitalism to be always and everywhere an easily exploitable "mass taste".

What Adorno finds most astonishing, however, is the contradiction between two facts. Firstly, the fact that many TV viewers, for example, do complain about the boringly repetitive and predictable programme of "entertainment" which they are offered, and which only presents to them in countless slight variations images of the happiness and adventure that their own lives lack. And secondly, the fact that these viewers nonetheless return to their TV sets regularly every night:

They insist unwaveringly on the ideology by which they are enslaved.[31]

When people seek refuge in the fictional films and TV series produced by the entertainment industry they do so, argues Adorno, in full awareness of what they are doing. Why do they opt in this way to hoodwink themselves, instead of going in search of a truly lived life? Adorno's answer here is, as so often, a bitterly disillusioning one:

The chances are that every citizen of the wrong world would find the right one unbearable; he would be too impaired for it.[32]

If Adorno is right, then, we surrender ourselves so uninhibitedly to the pleasures of the "false life" because we feel that we would no longer be up to the task of living any true one. Adorno even estimated his own chances of being able to live such a "true life" as very low. This is why his most personal book, the *Minima Moralia*, bears the highly significant subtitle Reflections from Damaged Life.

Negative Dialectics – Overcoming Language and Liberation from the Dictatorship of the Concept

There is one further fateful factor, argues Adorno, that runs as a red thread through the whole of human history. This is language. Because ever since the Stone Age human beings have been giving names to things and to other animals. We have named many animals, for example, in terms of the way that they have looked or sounded to us, calling a certain bird a "cuckoo" or a certain, apparently slow-moving animal a "sloth". But this practice of ordering the world around us in terms of separating and classifying words and notions, which may seem on first consideration to be something completely harmless, in fact leaves a profound mark on our whole way of thinking and tends to become, so argues Adorno, a dangerous "instrument of power". [33] Because, even if we are not aware of it, a claim to power or domination is indeed always latent, in more or less disguised form, in the concepts that we employ and in the words that express them:

Like the material tool [...] the concept is the idea-tool that fits into things at the very point from which one can take hold of them.[34]

Concepts, then, are, in Adorno's view, "idea-tools" by means of which we seize hold of the things of the world, set up Nature before ourselves and divide and label it in such a way that it can be dominated and manipulated by us. For example, the gardener draws such beings as caterpillars and snails under the common classifying term of "pests" so that, once labelled in this way, he will be better able to combat them with some "pesticide" produced especially for this purpose. Already latent, then, in the very concept "pest" is the subjective power-claim of human beings directed to the protection of their crops and other cultivated plants. For wild ducks, however, and other such creatures that nourish themselves on snails, and indeed for ecologically-minded humans for whom an intact food chain and a diversity of species are important concerns, snails and caterpillars are not "pests" at all but rather very useful beings. Thus concepts, Adorno argues, do not in the end reflect objective reality, let alone anything that we can call "the truth", but rather serve only subjective interests in domination.

"Conceptualizing" a thing, then, being always a subjective and a specifically targeted operation, never really does justice to the character of the thing conceptualized. By drawing a plant or an animal under the generic concept "pest" or "weed" what one really expresses is a power-interest: one which dictates that the plant or animal in question be destroyed. Caterpillar and dandelion are identified, respectively, by these two terms as representatives of a class of things that must be eliminated and thus as things which, considered on their own terms, they are not:

> [...] Identitarian thinking says what something comes under, what it exemplifies or represents and what, accordingly, it is not itself.[35]

In this way we brutally cram the frame of our concepts over the diversity of the world, regardless of whether these concepts actually fit the world or not. But since concepts and words always inflict in this way a kind of violence upon the object they are used to designate, our language itself is nothing other than a mechanism of domination, an accumulation of power-related subjective interests.

Thus, language and words have, since time immemorial, served the powerful as means of manipulation. It is not just in totalitarian states that we observe such phenomena as the deployment of concepts like "enemy of the people" or "class enemy" in order to demonize certain sections of the citizenry. Comparable linguistic manipulations occur, in more subtle ways, also in democracies. Thus, for example, after Germany had lost two world wars in succession the name "War Ministry", which had originally been applied to the section of the German government in charge of military matters, was scrapped. Germany remilitarized, indeed, even after the Second World War. But the concept used to name and think about this department of the government was henceforth "Ministry of Defence". Indeed, in the immediate post-war period it was even proposed that this Ministry be re-established under the name "Ministry of Peace".

The choice of these names, which was in each case at the same time the choice of a concept through which to understand the thing so named, was clearly intended to discourage or even prevent an otherwise obvious mental association: namely, that between the building-up and arming of an army and the notion of actually making war. In other words, it was a way of controlling and combating the great resistance to the idea of rearmament found in the war-weary German population after 1945.

It has been a perennial practice of politicians to use the power of names, and of the concepts that names define, to achieve their ends. The German Christian Democratic Party, for example, after having been heavily defeated by the Social Democratic Party in the parliamentary elections of 1972, established a party-internal "work-group on language". This group was tasked with finding a way to take the key concepts, "freedom", "justice" and "solidarity", that had helped the Social Democrats win the elections and to reflect these concepts in the Christian Democrats' programme so as to regain the advantage in political argument.

Some years later the Christian Democrats fought back to electoral victory using the slogan "Freedom, not socialism!" The chief political strategist of the party, Alfred Dregger, had very deliberately chosen just these two concepts to campaign on. The slogan strongly associated the Social Democrat leader Helmut Schmidt with the notion of a regression back to socialism and its planned economy while presenting Helmut Kohl, the Christian Democrat leader, as the embodiment of "freedom" and "progress". The strength of the association established between ideas here remained undiminished despite its having been, in historical fact, rather the Social Democrats who were, for more than a century, the main political force standing for these two values of freedom and progress. It is quite possible, then, to use words and concepts to manipulate, as in these specific cases of political self-presentation and propaganda.

Names and concepts, however, as Adorno further argues, exercise a still greater power, and this in a second, much wider context. Quite generally speaking, it is only within a framework established by them that names and concepts allow us to think at all. Whoever tries to clearly conceive of an idea without making use of some form of language in doing so will have immediately to recognize to what extent we find ourselves prisoners in the iron house formed by the words and sentences of whatever language we speak. Escape from such an "iron house" of names and concepts appears impossible. We are and remain therefore, argues Adorno, slaves of language and of its false names and concepts.

Adorno's sombre conclusion, then, is that what he calls the all-encompassing "entangling web of artificial blindness" does not consist, in the end, just in the dialectic of Enlightenment and in the scientific positivism to which this dialectic gave rise, nor even just in the capitalist economic and social system. Language too is a part, and an extremely dangerous part, of this "entangling web of artificial blindness". From the day of our birth onward, we live and move in a completely manipulated world and even our speech itself is an aspect and expression of this universal manipulation:

The whole is the false.[36]

But if "the whole" really is an entirely "false whole" and if we are all, as Adorno maintains, imprisoned within such an all-encompassing "entangling web of artificial blindness", then it follows logically that this imprisonment, and this induced blindness to the truth, must apply also to Adorno himself. The question, in other words, necessarily arises of how Adorno can possibly know that our universe is an entirely manipulated universe if, as follows from Adorno's own logic, he himself is a part of the "false whole"? Adorno would not be Adorno if he did not also have an answer to this question:

The physical moment tells our knowledge that suffering ought not to be, that things should be different.[37]

It is suffering, then, that signals even to the manipulated human faculty of reason that something is not as it should be and that we need to make things different from how they are. This is Adorno's explanation of why, despite the total manipulation that characterizes our world, we are nonetheless able to experience our false condition as indeed false. We do so simply because we suffer from it. But how, above and beyond the mere fact of suffering from this condition, can we actually know and analyse it as a false one? Adorno proposes that there be applied here the dialectical method of Critical Theory:

> To this end, dialectics is obliged to make a final move: being at once the impression and the critique of the entangling web of artificial blindness, it must now turn even against itself.[38]

What does this mean, concretely? We must, argues Adorno, come, through our dialectical thinking, to understand ourselves as being, at one and the same time, expressions of this "entangling web of artificial blindness" and agents capable of critiquing it. That is to say, each of us must become thesis and antithesis combined in a single individual. But this is only possible, he goes on, where we learn to turn, in a second movement, our critical thinking against ourselves. Concretely, this means that, after having completed a mental stocktaking of all that we hold to represent objective reality, we must then go on to train a certain critical suspicion upon our own selves. That is, we must confess to ourselves the possibility that everything that we believe we know might well be an illusion born of manipulation which needs, not just in its individual details but in its entirety, to be tested and verified once again from the bottom up.

Adorno's philosophical project, then, consists in a permanent criticism of thought by thought itself. It is only thanks to such permanent self-critique that we might have a chance of recognizing our false life as indeed just that: false. Adorno describes this important dialectical process, whereby the subject first constructs a world and then critically unmasks the construction, in extremely personal terms as something which he had felt, since his earliest youth, to be a kind of vocation:

To use the strength of the subject to break through the fallacy of constitutive subjectivity – this is what the author felt to be his task ever since he came to trust his own mental impulses.[39]

How, though, is it possible for the individual subject to "break through the fallacy", as Adorno puts it, of the subject's own construction of reality? Adorno gives us at least an indication as to how we might do this. We need to try to bring about a fundamental transformation in our perception, that is, in the whole way in which we arrive at what counts for us as "knowledge". All too often, as we have seen, the effort to "know" things is an effort just to find labels for them in order better to control them. And the labels found, such as "pest" or "weed", are often labels that do a kind of violence to the things known. The practice of "knowing" in this way, then, must be largely given up if knowledge is to be anything like true knowledge:

The true exertion of knowledge consists mainly in the dismantling of its usual exertion, which is violence against the object.[40]

A "true exertion" of human cognitive powers, in other words, and a true knowledge of the object, arise only where:

The subject tears through the veil that the subject himself has woven around the object. And the subject

can do this only where, passively but without fear, entrusts himself to his own experience.[41]

But such a "passive" experience of the truth of the object, which is a truth lying beyond all concepts and beyond the claims to mastery implied in concepts, is something that is difficult to achieve and even more difficult to describe. This experience of a "truth beyond concepts", argues Adorno, is certainly no easy thing to communicate. It exists, however, none the less. At this point Adorno's critique is directed against the fact that we nowadays tend to accept nothing as "true" that cannot be put into words and communicated. There is, however, Adorno argues, beyond this kind of truth a truth that escapes every sort of communication but exists nonetheless:

Direct communicability to everyone is not a criterion of truth. We must resist the all but universal

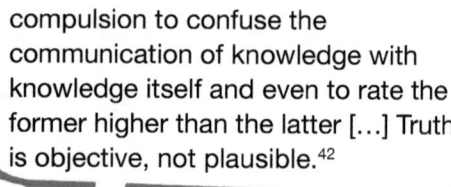

compulsion to confuse the communication of knowledge with knowledge itself and even to rate the former higher than the latter [...] Truth is objective, not plausible.[42]

Truth is objectively possible, even when it is of such a kind that it can no longer be plausibly communicated to a conversation partner. And now Adorno draws a radical conclusion. It is the destiny, and indeed the true vocation, of philosophy to have to generate truths which escape the domination of conceptual thinking and are, consequently, no longer to be directly expressed in words and most definitely not to be "expounded" in the formal and systematic way in which philosophy has traditionally been expounded:

Essentially [...] philosophy is not expoundable. If it were, it would be superfluous. The fact that most of it can be expounded speaks against it.[43]

Of What Use Is Adorno's Discovery for Us Today?

Truth Beyond Words – Can One Think Conceptually Against the Concept?

Adorno's critique of language and of ways of thinking bound to language surely opened up yet another new dimension in philosophy. But if not just our capitalist economy, our technocratic structures of administration and our positivistic natural sciences but even the very language we use in order to articulate our thoughts are all expressions of the dominion of a "false condition", then the project specifically of a critical philosophy appears much more difficult even than the basic philosophical enterprise itself. Here, two decisive questions necessarily arise: namely, 'is there a truth beyond words?' and if so, 'how can one hope to draw nearer to this truth without having recourse either to concepts or to modes of thought already (de)formed by language?'

Traditionally, philosophy had always attempted to grasp truth through concepts and sum up reality in the form of communicated propositions. No one seriously claiming to be a philosopher has ever published as his *magnum opus* a book consisting of nothing but empty pages. But, if philosophy in the form of "Critical Theory" is really to take a stance of emancipatory opposition, as Adorno envisages it doing, to that violence and domination which is inherent even in language, then the philosopher is faced with the task of renouncing all conceptualization and yet still somehow summing up a truth that is lost as soon as it is spoken. It is indeed such an utterly paradoxical performance on the part of the philosopher that Adorno demands:

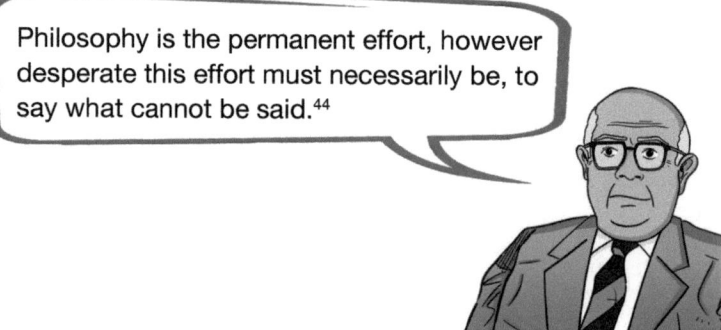

Philosophy is the permanent effort, however desperate this effort must necessarily be, to say what cannot be said.[44]

What Adorno is envisaging here seems initially to be a hopeless paradox. At first sight, this "saying of the unsayable" appears to be a pure impossibility. It cannot, one might think, be reasonably demanded of the philosopher that he refrain from using words and propositions as he becomes aware of the violence that linguistic expression does to all that it expresses. The philosopher, it would appear, cannot get around the simple dilemma: "either you use words to say what you want to say about the objective world, and put up with the violence that words necessarily do to this latter, or you say nothing at all." Adorno is fully aware of this dilemma. But he holds nonetheless to the paradoxical aim he has set himself:

> The cognitive utopia would be to use concepts to unseal the non-conceptual with concepts without making it their equal.[45]

What can Adorno possibly mean when he speaks here of "unsealing the non-conceptual with concepts without making it their equal"? He means that, although we do indeed have no choice but to go on thinking in concepts if we are to go on thinking at all, we should nonetheless not immediately slap the "labels" of pre-existing words and notions onto all that we recognize to be true and wish to express as such. Rather, Adorno recommends a much subtler practice of circling and thinking around the object of our thought as the sole appropriate way of approaching it without destroying it. The name that Adorno gives to this more subtle and distanced way of evoking what we hold to be true is "mimesis".

The notion of mimesis is absolutely central to Adorno's final philosophical statement, the *Negative Dialectics*, and indeed to all his later, most defining work. The term is Greek and means, essentially, "imitation". Although the Greek philosophers used it mostly in writing on the arts, Adorno gives it a much broader application covering the history of the human species in all its fields of activity. Because, Adorno argues, already millennia before the emergence of art and artists in any distinct and recognizable form, prehistoric Man had used practices of imitation to understand the world around him and to make life within it liveable.

Primitive peoples crafted magical masks, for example, in order to evoke by imitation both those objects and events in the natural world that delighted them and those that terrified them. Masks of various mighty animals were used to summon good fortune in the hunt, or the vitality required to carry it off successfully. Plant-masks were used to summon fertility and death-masks to ease people's path into the world beyond. By imitating what was desired or feared a certain distance was taken from it, so that the objective world could be better come to terms with by the emerging human subject and many a truth processed and worked through which could neither be understood conceptually nor communicated in words.

Today, the arts have become the heirs of these prehistoric mimetic practices. Like the ancient rituals that evoked the forces of Nature through their respectful imitation, the arts today, while representing and expressing something which touches and moves us, do so without using words in any directly communicative sense and thus without compelling us to "conceptualize" the represented or expressed thing in a way that deprives it of its magic. In works of art, Adorno contends, things can be "said" that could never be expressed by the use of theoretical concepts or by the words of language used as they are normally used. The magic of art consists also in the fact that what is "gotten across" in an artwork is never anything competing for the title of being the "scientific truth":

Art is magic delivered from the lie of being truth.[46]

Adorno is trying, then, through his demand that philosophy should transcend, mimetically, the limits of conceptual thought, to make us more sensitive to the need to seek experiences and perceptions that lie outside the sphere of strictly logical thinking and to accept the validity also of these experiences.

In his *Aesthetic Theory*, his last great statement that remained uncompleted when he died of a heart attack at the age of 65, Adorno attempted to trace out this line of investigation even further. It is astonishing that a brilliant rhetorician and linguistic virtuoso like Adorno, who juggled words and lines of argument with unsurpassable skill, should have attempted, towards the end of his life, to pass beyond the limits of linguistically-mediated thought itself.

This is perhaps to be explained by the fact that he was a passionate lover of music and himself the composer of many musical pieces. Philosophy and music were deeply interwoven, indeed inseparable, in

Adorno's mind. He saw, in fact, philosophy's greatest challenge to consist in the very same problem as music's greatest challenge did: namely, that of finding a way to express its own "suspended state":

(Philosophy's) suspended state is nothing but the expression of its own inexpressibility. In this respect it is a true sister of music.[47]

"To express the inexpressible", then, is Adorno's great dialectical postulate. There can be no doubt but that, with such ambitions, he carried the "critical theory of society" as far as it is humanly possible to carry it. He developed critiques, as "tools of domination", of Enlightenment, positivism, the natural sciences, capitalism, the mass entertainment that he called the "culture industry", and finally even language itself.

But when a real mass movement of resistance to domination began, in the form of the student movement of the late 1960s that brought thousands of young people onto the streets in protest against the ossified authoritarian structures of post-war German and other societies, Adorno chose not to join them but rather to continue to labour away in his study on the complex problems raised by his *Aesthetic Theory*. He had, indeed, sympathy and understanding for the concerns and demands of the students, many of whom made explicit reference in their pamphlets and speeches to the critique of capitalism developed in Adorno's writings. But he consistently refused to take on the leadership role in the movement that many urged on him or even to take part in any of the demonstrations and rallies that took place almost daily on the campus of Frankfurt University in those tumultuous years of 1968 and 1969. In a letter to his former colleague Marcuse who, from his own academic position on the West Coast of the USA, was offering a far more active support to the student movement that reached its culmination in that year, he expressed very serious reservations about this activism that claimed to be only a consistent development of ideas he himself had taught:

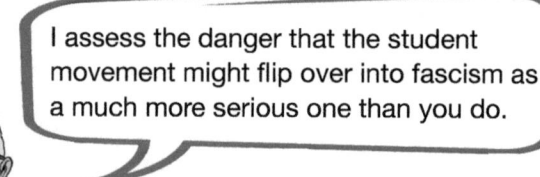

I assess the danger that the student movement might flip over into fascism as a much more serious one than you do.

You only have to look into the manically frozen eyes of those who are, even while citing our writings, turning their fury on us.[48]

Adorno was not speaking merely theoretically here. The students of 1968 did in fact turn their anger on him on more than one occasion. As it became evident that he was refusing to give unconditional support to the agitation his own lectures began to be disrupted by the activists. Perhaps the most notorious, and most grotesque, of these targeted disruptions was the "Naked Breasts Action". After several minutes of vain appeals to the students to either allow the lecture to be held or vacate the lecture hall Adorno himself was finally driven from the room by three young women who charged, with bared breasts, onto the podium and began to execute a pantomime of kissing, caressing and bombarding the old philosopher with flowers. All that remained was a mocking rhyme already chalked up on the board by an agitator before the start of this abortive lecture: "If we let Adorno have his way, then capitalism's here to stay". In the leaflets and pamphlets distributed by the students around the university the personal invective against the ageing philosopher was often even more violent. "Let him jabber away to empty lecture halls," ran one, "until he's 'adorned himself' to death."

Adorno, then, was certainly no "man of action". This should have been obvious from an incident that took place very early on in the '68 "revolt" when his status as an idol of the students was still untarnished. As he passed through one of the university auditoriums where a group of activist students happened to have gathered for one of their countless "discussion sessions" the presence of the great Critical Theorist was noticed by some among their number and gradually the whole group burst into applause. The clapping was an unmistakable invitation to Adorno to take over the microphone at the front of the hall and speak words of encouragement, or at least words of some sort, to the young activists. For a moment Adorno appeared on the point of taking up this invitation, as he continued to walk slowly toward the front of the hall. At the last moment, however, he vanished into a side-exit leading to the placid, book-lined offices of the Philosophy Department, leaving the applause of his revolutionary admirers to die out without result.

Must Enlightenment and Science Really Always End in Totalitarianism?

But to what extent is Adorno's Critical Theory in its broadest sense still of use and relevance for us today? Was he correct in his central theses? Does the movement of Enlightenment, along with the triumphal march of the natural sciences and modern technocracy that it ushered in, really bear a part of the responsibility for the racism of the 20th century? And above all: is there a risk that reason, where it takes the form of merely "instrumental reason", will flip over once again into a new irrationalism? Adorno's own position here is unmistakable:

Millions of innocent people [...] were systematically murdered. That cannot be dismissed by any living person as a superficial phenomenon, as an

aberration from the course of history to be disregarded when compared to the great dynamic of progress, of enlightenment, of the supposed growth of humanitarianism.[49]

The planned annihilation of human beings, Adorno contends here, cannot possibly be minimized or dismissed as a mere passing deviation from the highroad of steadily progressing Enlightenment and humanization but must rather, realistically, be understood as an essential constituent part of modern civilization itself. Turkey's massacre of a million Armenians during the First World War was also, Adorno points out, no mere unhappy accident but rather the planned-out consequence of a new ethnically-based self-conception that emerged in many nations during that century. Only if we investigate and understand the true causes of the barbaric acts committed in the 20th century can we hope to prevent further genocides. It must be recognized that such ideological reflexes are still present in us today:

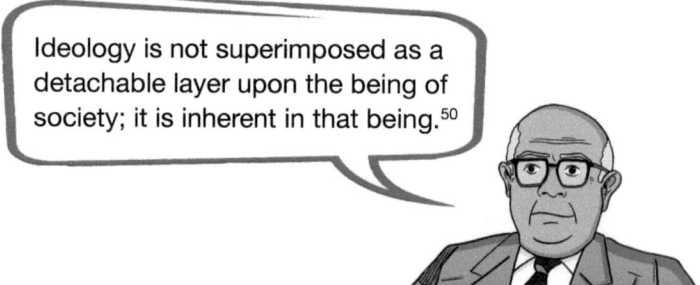

Ideology is not superimposed as a detachable layer upon the being of society; it is inherent in that being.[50]

Our only hope of preventing the emergence of further racist movements is a constant vigilance and a constant readiness to critique the traits in our own characters susceptible of being seduced by authoritarianism. Though to break radically, indeed, with the "false condition" in which we have been raised is, so runs Adorno's pessimistic prognosis, due to the dialectic of Enlightenment and the systematic ideological indoctrination of capitalism completely impossible:

Wrong life cannot be lived rightly.[51]

Another great figure of 20th-century critical social philosophy, the Marxist theoretician Georg Lukacs, harshly criticized Adorno for just this attitude. With his complete rejection of the optimism of the Enlightenment era, so objected Lukacs, Adorno had withdrawn into a kind of self-created "comfort zone" of complacent inactivity. If one is convinced, Lukacs pointed out, that it is in very principle impossible to extricate oneself from the "false whole", then clearly it makes no sense to involve oneself in any attempt to bring about actual social change. With their combination of profound pessimism and complacent inactivity Adorno and his fellow Frankfurt School theorists had, in Lukacs's deeply sarcastic characterization of them, taken up residence in "the Grand Hotel 'Abyss' ".

Also the philosopher generally perceived to have been Adorno's intellectual heir in critical social theory, Habermas, felt the pessimism displayed by the first generation of the Frankfurt School as regards the inevitable failure of Enlightenment to have been unjustifiably extreme. "How can these two men of the Enlightenment," asks Habermas about Adorno and Horkheimer, "be so unappreciative of the rational content of modernity that all they perceive everywhere is a binding of reason and domination, of power and validity?" [52]

The criticisms levelled against Adorno's position by Lukacs and by Habermas may well be partly justified. It remains, however, inarguably the case that Adorno, with his profound suspicion regarding the rationalism of the Enlightenment, made an essential contribution to our understanding of fascism and totalitarianism. He was surely not wrong in contending that, after the collapse of the mythical and religious world-picture and in the course of the Enlightenment that followed, there has arisen a dangerous new faith in science which can at any moment flip over into a new irrationalism. Already Nietzsche had noted that human beings were finding it impossible to deal with the agonizing, valueless vacuum which had come into being after "the death of God". In place of God, Nietzsche had argued, human beings had begun to venerate new "idols" in the form not only of the promises of universal salvation through the "hard sciences" exposed by Adorno and Horkheimer but also of such pseudo-scientific world-explanations as socialism, nationalism, anti-Semitism and capitalism. Darwinism's mis-extrapolation into racism and chauvinism is just one example of this.

The hypothesis advanced by professors of such pseudo-disciplines as "Racial Science" whereby the "Aryan race" stands out as "superior" to all others had, as we know, horrible consequences. Adorno's philosophy sharpens our vigilance, a vigilance especially necessary in a world which has seen such horrors, with regard to "scientific" theories, reminding us to analyse them closely with an eye to establishing whether they really consist of rationally legitimate elements which are of service to society or whether they represent only dangerous ideological promises of salvation which finally culminate in a lapse back into barbaric irrationalism. Adorno displays especial scepticism in the face of scientists who claim to be able to derive from the positive facts of Nature that they establish prescriptions as to how people ought to act in society.

The Whole is Not Falsifiable – Adorno's Critique of Popper and of Positivism

Adorno critiques the natural sciences and their methods on account of their lack of reflection about themselves and the narrow way of looking at the world that results from this. Scientists, argues Adorno, allow nothing to count as "true" except what they can grasp, establish and measure in the external world and can reproduce in empirically-based experiments. But this means that they render themselves blind, right from the start and basis of their undertakings, to every type of truth which is of a complex and less materially measurable nature.

It is also often the case that scientists refuse to admit to themselves that their scientific studies are necessarily performed from the compelling perspective of certain power-related calculations, such as the goals set by large corporations or the broader, more long-term interests of the capitalist class ruling the societies in which these scientific studies are carried out. Only a "Critical Theory", so Adorno and Horkheimer contended, was in a position to identify and analyse these specific interests that lay, in fact, behind all seemingly disinterested scientific enquiry. Defenders of these non-reflective sciences, however, replied to this critique of the philosophers with a counter-critique of their own: philosophy, it was retorted, had no right to critique science because it was itself no more than unprovable speculation.

These two approaches, the philosophy of knowledge propounded by Critical Theory and the theory of knowledge based directly on the methods of the natural sciences themselves, had been on a collision course with one another ever since Critical Theory was first developed long before World War Two. But things came to a head only in 1961 at a conference of the German Sociological Association. The two keynote speakers at this conference, Adorno and the Austrian philosopher Karl Popper, became involved in a heated debate about the task and the methods of sociology which was remembered as "the Positivist dispute in German sociology" and which still excites great interest today.

Popper, whose training had been in the fields of physics and mathematics as well as in that of philosophy, opened the conference by presenting twenty-seven theses on "the logic of the social sciences". His presentation caused a sensation, above all with its demand that the social sciences too should, in future, learn to work using the basic defining research methods of the natural sciences as he, Popper, conceived of these.

In the famous sixth thesis of these twenty-seven, for example, Popper called on the social sciences to proceed, thenceforth, in exactly the same way that, on his view, the natural sciences did: i.e. by advancing distinct, individual hypotheses which would then have to be empirically verified by really established events, facts and measurements or, in the absence of these, rejected as false.

If a hypothesis were proven to be false or, in Popper's preferred terminology, "falsified", then it had to be dropped and replaced by some other, better explanatory model. Thus, the hypothesis "all swans are white" would remain a valid hypothesis only up to the point where someone would discover a black swan, this latter discovery "falsifying" the hypothesis. In this way, science acquires ever newer and more precise explanatory models and thereby an ever higher level of knowledge.

But what if one proceeds as we have seen Adorno do: i.e. not by distinct and individual critical statements but rather by a critique that explicitly embraces "the whole", advancing the hypothesis that the experience of Man under capitalism is a negative experience in its entirety and in its every detail? It is clear that such a critique and such hypotheses must be, on the terms established by Popper, unscientific and thus completely inadmissible as "social science" in any valid sense.

It is plainly impossible to measure, critique, verify or falsify the hypothesis that without capitalism there would be a better solution of the problem of human coexistence and, as Popper argues, "if a proposed solution is not open to pertinent criticism, then it is excluded as unscientific." [53] The position of the Critical Theorists, then, was an unscientific position from the very outset.

Adorno, however, who gave his speech immediately after Popper's, levelled an equally harsh criticism against this latter. Popper, he claimed, was betraying the true task of sociology by limiting sociological research to small sub-regions of society and to empirically verifiable bodies of facts:

If its concepts are to be true, critical sociology is, according to its own idea, necessarily also a critique of society.[54]

For Adorno, the true task of sociology consists precisely in recognizing society as a whole for what it is. It consists, in other words, in analysing the structural connection – namely, the capitalist system – which binds all society's parts together and thereby exerts a massive effect on our social life and on the lives of all individuals. It makes no sense, Adorno argued, to investigate such distinct sociological categories as "family", "authorities", "peer groups" or "mass media" without critiquing the general form of society which mobilizes these as its "psycho-social agencies" and thereby essentially makes them what they are. Popper's intention, he went on, was to prescribe for sociology a concentration on certain "falsifiable" individual aspects of the social whole. But such a methodology could never hope to uncover the actual causes of society's being the way it is, let alone provide the tools for changing it.

Furthermore, Adorno went on, all the supposed data that a social scientist proceeding in Popper's positivistic manner attempts to establish merely empirically are, in reality, pseudo-facts already manipulated and deformed by the "false" social reality in which we live. It is all the more important, then, for the social scientist to consider every phenomenon he investigates in the light of this "false whole", something that only Critical Theory can achieve. Even the natural sciences, indeed, lapse inevitably, since they lack the moment of self-critique, back into their own closed world of concepts:

The blindness and muteness of the data to which positivism reduces the world passes over into language itself, which is limited to registering those data.[55]

In short, then, it is Adorno's contention that the positivistically registering and manipulating experimental thinking typical of the natural sciences cannot and must not be carried over into the social sciences and into philosophy. Philosophy, indeed, is distinguished precisely by the fact that it goes beyond the natural sciences by

> [...] representing that, within human thinking, that is not 'the concept' in the instrumental sense, that does not manipulate or categorize. To this extent, there does indeed exist an affinity between philosophy and art.[56]

Can 'Wrong Life Be Lived Rightly' After All?

The great question that every reader asks himself after reading Adorno's work is: is there any way at all, in the end, out of the "all-entangling web of artificial blindness" that Adorno describes? Are we really irredeemably manipulated prisoners within a "false life"? Or does there exist a chance for us of recognizing the false condition for what it is and of escaping from it? And if there is not, is a philosophy like Adorno's of any use to us at all?

Adorno himself was often asked whether the Critical Theory he had developed could have any sense at all if, all critique notwithstanding, each of us remained condemned to lead a "false life". Adorno certainly finds himself in a dilemma here, because the two radical thoughts that form the core of his philosophy – "the whole is the false" and "wrong life cannot be lived rightly" – seem necessarily, when they are related one to the other, to have to place Adorno's whole emancipatory project in question. But Adorno was aware of this, of course, and sometimes raised the problem, in his teaching, himself. For example, right at the start of one of the courses he gave at Frankfurt University on *Problems of Moral Philosophy*, he said to his students:

When you attend a course of lectures given by someone who has written a book on the good

– or rather the bad – life, it is reasonable to assume that you [...] have come in the hope that these lectures will teach you something about this good life.[57]

And Adorno did in fact go on, in these lectures, to try to resolve to some extent, at least, the dilemma we have referred to above. It is indeed impossible, he conceded, to formulate in the present day, with a good conscience, any notion of "the good life" that would be valid for society as a whole or even just for the individual. Both Hegel and Marx, he went on to admit, had been far too optimistic when they had construed human history as a continuous ascent and progress toward their respective social-philosophical ideals of a reconciliation of the World Spirit with itself and a classless society. After Auschwitz, such was Adorno's firm conviction, it had become morally irresponsible to predict any such thoroughly dialectical development of human history toward a final goal consisting in one or another sort of "true and good life".

Nor did there any longer exist, Adorno believed, a credible blueprint for how an individual could live such a "true and good life" just for him- or herself. We do find Adorno proposing in these lectures, however, two ways of proceeding which might improve, to some degree, the life of the individual and help him or her to resist, at least to some extent, the pressure of our "false condition". The first of these ways of proceeding consists in a kind of "living as if...":

One should live, so far as this is humanly possible, in the way that one believes it would be right for a person to live in a world freed from the

constraints of this presently existing one [...] One should, in other words, attempt to anticipate in one's own presently-lived life, even in the face of all the inevitable contradictions and conflicts that this will involve, that form of existence which is in fact the only right one.[58]

But what does this mean, concretely? It can only mean to live, right now, as if one's own personal utopia had already been brought to realization. If my vision, in other words, is one of the abolition of a money-based economy, then I should live, right at this moment, without money, acquiring the things I need to live by exchanging other concrete goods for them, or simply taking what I need, without paying, from the shelves of supermarkets. Adorno's "living as if..." could also mean that, if I were a vegan, I would look on the accordance to animals of the full measure of their rights, and quite especially the inviolability of their lives, as already a reality and would condemn butchers, and indeed all meat-eaters, as murderers. It could also mean, and this was something that Adorno himself surely practiced, anticipating that total liberation of society's libido that Critical Theory saw as being one day possible and openly carrying on, already in the present day and in one's own life, affairs with young students, models and other women.

So far so good. It becomes a more difficult matter, however, in the case where an individual or a group of individuals resolves to live in our present day as if the potential future redistribution of capital had already really been brought about. There are, indeed, models in history for such visionary projects: Robin Hood and his fellow outlaws, for example, who acted as if the redistribution of wealth from the rich to the poor were something entirely legal. But it is very clear that this "living as if…" that Adorno recommends must lead, sooner or later, to conflicts. Adorno, moreover, was fully aware of this:

Such an aspiration is necessarily condemned to failure and to contradiction but one has no choice but to live this contradiction through to the bitter end.

The most important of the forms taken by this in our present day is: resistance.[59]

This question, then, of "how wrong life can be lived rightly" is answered, initially, by Adorno with an urging of us to bring our own utopias stubbornly to realization even in the face of all resistances. One must, as an individual living in the world as it exists, nonetheless live one's life "in the way that one believes it would be right for a person to live in a world freed from the constraints of this presently existing one". In addition to this he gives a further, more cautious hint as to what the "right life" might be after all:

The only thing that one can, perhaps, say here is that 'living rightly' today exists in the form of a resistance to the forms of false life, once they have been seen through and recognized as false.[60]

Only through resistance to "the forms of false life, once they have been seen through and recognized as false" can one take even a step, says Adorno, toward "life lived rightly". One might thereby, under certain circumstances, compel the world and oneself to take a new direction even if one does not already have a concrete vision of "life lived rightly" in mind. Dialectical thinkers like Adorno speak here of "determinate negation":

[...] Utopia inheres in any case [...] in the determinate negation of that which merely 'is the case' and which, in and through its proving concretely to be something false, always at the same time points to a world as it ought to be.[61]

Thus it can, for example, make sense to become active in the movement opposing nuclear power even when one cannot propose any practical alternative as regards meeting energy-production needs. Because the danger alone that nuclear waste disposed of wrongly or unsuccessfully might result in radiation contamination lasting centuries is enough in itself to justify resistance. If such resistance proves successful, then there must necessarily occur, in a second step, a search for alternative sources of energy.

Also in one's private life it can sometimes be reasonable to engage in such determinate negation without having in mind any concrete alternative to what one negates. If a job, or a human relationship, are becoming unbearable it is absolutely necessary to put an end to them, even if it cannot yet be foreseen just what will take their place. To quote an old German proverb: "There's nowhere you won't find something you'll prefer to death". If Adorno is right, it is only through direct negation that there can emerge an altered situation that might bring with it new possibilities.

The Power of Negative Thinking – Negation That Finds No Rest in Any Affirmation

Here we find ourselves face to face once again with the central idea of Adorno's *Negative Dialectics*: it is possible, indeed urgently needful, to engage in an activity of negation that is endlessly sustained and finds no rest, at any point, in any correspondent act of affirmation:

> (What I have to teach) consists in the outlines of a philosophy which neither presupposes the notion of an identity of being with thinking nor culminates

> in such a notion but which aims rather to articulate the very opposite notion to this: namely, the way that concept and thing, subject and object, necessarily tend to point away from one another and must therefore remain unreconciled.[62]

By saying that Critical Theory is a philosophy, or the "outlines of a philosophy", which "does not culminate in the notion of identity" Adorno means that his thought is such that it does not and never will flow out into any optimistic idea of one-ness and of "same embracing same". In this respect, his thinking is radically different from that of Plato, who urges us to meld into mental unity with the Idea of the Good, the True and the Beautiful, and from that of Hegel, who foresees a complete reconciliation, in the end, of individual with society and of mind with matter. It is even radically different from that of Marx, whose philosophy of history terminated in the idea of a completely classless, completely reconciled and unified society. Adorno, by contrast, wants to preserve and maintain precisely the moment of unreconciledness. For him, philosophy means a

[...] negation of negation that will not become a positing.[63]

Adorno demands of us – and this is the innermost core of his philosophy – a permanent non-identity and permanent endurance of the non-identical. This is not an easy thing, because normally human beings long for, and aspire to, reconciliation and identity.

Thus, for example, the commonly-cited notion of "ego identity" suggests that we can and should come to terms with ourselves and make of ourselves a single harmonious unity: precisely a "same embracing same". Every time our ideal image of ourselves and our actual lived reality begin to drift apart from one another, this is experienced as a so-called "identity crisis". And when we speak of a "balanced personality" or of an intact "ego identity" this means, concretely, that the ideal image that we form of our own personality concords with what we really are, what we really succeed in achieving, and what we see reflected back to us from the perceptions of others. But such an identity, such a perfect concordance, argues Adorno, would not be something to be wished for even if it could be achieved. One must, on the contrary, remain always in a stance of negation, above all vis-à-vis one's own self, so as not to become complacent, self-satisfied and blind both to one's own problems and to the problems of the world around one:

It lies in the definition of negative dialectics that it will not come to rest in itself [...] [64]

But of the greatest importance of all is the aspect of the individual's non-identity with society. The fascist slogan "one empire, one people, one leader" sums up very graphically the dangers lurking in the ideal of a total harmony, a total identity between individual and social system. In Adorno's terms, such a total harmony is tantamount to the individual's being surrendered up to the "false whole". It is only if we succeed, Adorno believed, in maintaining our own non-identity in the face of that totality that is represented by any and every society, only if we remain permanently critical and "negative" vis-à-vis co-optation by the culture industry, the economic system and all the envies and resentments that arise from these, that we can hope to prevent the re-establishment, in future, of totalitarian systems:

The almost insoluble task is to let neither the power of others, nor our own powerlessness, stupefy us.[65]

The power of negative thinking is not to be underestimated. Adorno showed us this power more clearly, and urged us to hold true to it more strongly, than any other thinker before or since. He was, himself, a past master of all forms of critique and perhaps the greatest and most consistent cultural pessimist who ever lived. At bottom, however, his message was that, for all our alienation and for all the massive co-optation of the individual by the "false whole", there always remains to us this negative force of critique as an instrument of liberation.

We cannot, indeed, just shake off what Adorno calls "the whole". But we can, in our non-identity with this latter, preserve and maintain our openness: an openness for that which always survives as a remainder once the closed equation of "the whole" has been worked out to its end, for that which eludes the grasp of conceptual thinking and which forms, for just this reason, an essential part of our humanity. Even in a manipulated world there still persists a chance of freedom and of satisfaction of basic human needs. This chance persists in the form of resistance against that which has been recognized to be false and in the act of critical thinking itself:

Whatever has once been thought can be suppressed, forgotten, can vanish. But it cannot be denied that something of it survives.[66]

Bibliographical References

1   Theodor Adorno, Negative Dialectics, translated by E. B. Ashton, Seabury Press, New York, 1973, p. 320.

2   Theodor Adorno, Education After Auschwitz in Can One Live After Auschwitz ? A Philosophical Reader, edited by Rolf Tiedemann, Stanford University Press, Stanford, California, p. 22.

3   Theodor Adorno, Minima Moralia, Reflections on a Damaged Life, translated by E. F. N Jephcott, Verso Books, London, 2005, p. 50.

4   Max Horkheimer and Theodor W. Adorno, The Dialectic of Enlightenment: Philosophical Fragments, Stanford University Press, Stanford California 2002, p. 1.

5   Ibid. p. 6

6   Theodor Adorno, Minima Moralia, Reflections on a Damaged Life, translated by E. F. N Jephcott, Verso Books, London, 2005, p. 50.

7   Theodor Adorno, Soziologische Schriften I, Volume 8 of the Suhrkamp edition of the Gesammelte Schriften (Collected Writings), Suhrkamp Publishers, Frankfurt am Main 1979, p. 369 (no English edition of this text yet exists).

8   Theodor Adorno, Minima Moralia, Reflections on a Damaged Life, translated by E. F. N Jephcott, Verso Books, London, 2005, p. 39.

9   Theodor Adorno, Education After Auschwitz in Can One Live After Auschwitz ? A Philosophical Reader, edited by Rolf Tiedemann, Stanford University Press, Stanford, California, p. 14.

10 Max Horkheimer and Theodor W. Adorno, The Dialectic of Enlightenment: Philosophical Fragments, p. 6

11 Max Horkheimer and Theodor W. Adorno, The Dialectic of Enlightenment: Philosophical Fragments, p. 8.

12 Ibid. p. 9.

13 Ibid.

14 Theodor Adorno, Education After Auschwitz in Can One Live After Auschwitz ? A Philosophical Reader, edited by Rolf Tiedemann, Stanford University Press, Stanford, California, p. 17.

15 Theodor Adorno, Minima Moralia, Reflections on a Damaged Life, translated by E. F. N Jephcott, Verso Books, London, 2005, p. 40.

16 Ibid. p. 35.

17   Ibid. p. 53.

18   Ibid. p. 45.

19   Ibid. p. 37.

20   Ibid. p. 48.

21   La Mettrie, Man A Machine, Open Court Publishing Company, Chicago 1974, p. 93.

22   D'Holbach, System of Nature, J. P Mendum, Boston, 1889, p. 11.

23   Marquis de Sade, Justine, Philosophy in the Bedroom and Other Writings, Grove Press, New York, 1965, p.88

24   Max Horkheimer and Theodor W. Adorno, The Dialectic of Enlightenment: Philosophical Fragments, p. 74.

25   Ibid. p. 76.

26   Marquis de Sade, Justine, Philosophy in the Bedroom and Other Writings, Grove Press, New York, 1965, p. 296. The phrase occurs as the title of a manifesto read out by one of the characters in the midst of an orgy.

27   Ibid. p. 76, p. 76 and passim (Justine).

28   Max Horkheimer and Theodor W. Adorno, The Dialectic of Enlightenment: Philosophical Fragments, p. 74.

28   Ibid. p. 74.

29   Ibid. p. 112.

30   Ibid. p. 106.

31   Ibid.

32   Theodor Adorno, Negative Dialectics, translated by E. B. Ashton, Seabury Press, New York, 1973, p. 352.

33   Max Horkheimer and Theodor W. Adorno, The Dialectic of Enlightenment: Philosophical Fragments, p. 31.

34   Ibid.

35   Theodor Adorno, Negative Dialectics, translated by E. B. Ashton, Seabury Press, New York, 1973, p. 149.

36   Theodor Adorno, Minima Moralia, Reflections on a Damaged Life, translated by E. F. N Jephcott, Verso Books, London, 2005, p. 50.

37   Theodor Adorno, Negative Dialectics, translated by E. B. Ashton, Seabury Press, New York, 1973, p. 203.

38   Ibid. p. 406 (translation slightly revised).

39   Ibid. p. xx (Preface)

40   Adorno, Critical Models : Interventions and Catchwords, translated by Henry W. Pickford, Columbia University Press, 1998, p. 254,

translation revised.

41   Ibid. translation revised

42   Theodor Adorno, Negative Dialectics, translated by E. B. Ashton,
     Seabury Press, New York, 1973, p. 41.

43   Ibid. p. 34.

44   Theodor Adorno, Philosophische Terminologie, Volume 1,
     Suhrkamp Publishing House, Frankfurt am Main, 1979, p. 82
     (no English edition of this text yet exists).

45   Theodor Adorno, Negative Dialectics, translated by E. B. Ashton,
     Seabury Press, New York, 1973, p. 10.

46   Theodor Adorno, Minima Moralia, Reflections on a Damaged Life,
     translated by E. F. N Jephcott, Verso Books, London, 2005, p. 222.

47   Theodor Adorno, Negative Dialectics, translated by E. B. Ashton,
     Seabury Press, New York, 1973, p. 109.

48   Theodor Adorno, 1968 letter to Herbert Marcuse, cited in Wolfgang
     Kraushaar (ed.) Frankfurter Schule und Studentenbewegung,
     Zweitausendeins Publishers, Hamburg, 1998, Vol. 2, p. 652.

49   Theodor Adorno, Education After Auschwitz in Can One Live After
     Auschwitz ? A Philosophical Reader, edited by Rolf Tiedemann,
     Stanford University Press, Stanford, California, p. 14.

50   Theodor Adorno, Negative Dialectics, translated by E. B. Ashton,
     Seabury Press, New York, 1973, p. 354.

51   Theodor Adorno, Minima Moralia, Reflections on a Damaged Life,
     translated by E. F. N Jephcott, Verso Books, London, 2005, p. 39.

52   Juergen Habermas, The Philosophical Discourse of Modernity,
     translated by Frederick Lawrence, Polity Press, Cambridge, 1987,
     p. 121.

53   Theodor W. Adorno and others, The Positivist Dispute in German
     Sociology, translated by Glyn Adey and David Frisby, Heinemann
     Educational Books, London, 1976, p. 89

54   Ibid. p. 114.

55   Max Horkheimer and Theodor W. Adorno, The Dialectic of
     Enlightenment: Philosophical Fragments Stanford University Press,
     Stanford California 2002, pp. 133-134

56   Theodor Adorno, Philosophische Terminologie, Volume One, Suhrkamp
     Publishing House, Frankfurt am Main, 1979, p. 86 (no English edition
     of this text yet exists).

57   Theodor Adorno, Problems of Moral Philosophy, translated by Rodney

Livingstone, Stanford University Press, Stanford, California, 2001, p. 1.

58 Theodor W. Adorno, Probleme der Moralphilosophie, lecture delivered at Frankfurt University in the winter semester of 1956/57.

59 Ibid.

60 Theodor Adorno, Problems of Moral Philosophy, translated by Rodney Livingstone, Stanford University Press, Stanford, California, 2001, p. 187.

61 Theodor Adorno, in Gespraeche mit Ernst Bloch, edited by Rainer Traub and Harald Wieser, Suhrkamp Publishers, Frankfurt am Main, 1975, p. 70 (no English edition of this text yet exists).

62 Theodor Adorno, Vorlesung ueber Negative Dialektik in Volume 16 of the Suhrkamp edition of the Nachgelassene Schriften (Posthumous Writings), p. 15 ff. (no English edition of this text yet exists).

63 Theodor Adorno, Negative Dialectics, translated by E. B. Ashton, Seabury Press, New York, 1973, p. 406.

64 Ibid.

65 Theodor Adorno, Minima Moralia, Reflections on a Damaged Life, translated by E. F. N Jephcott, Verso Books, London, 2005, p. 57.

66 Adorno, Critical Models : Interventions and Catchwords, translated by Henry W. Pickford, Columbia University Press, 1998, p. 293.

Already published in the same series:

Walther Ziegler
Camus in 60 Minutes
ISBN 9783741227738

Walther Ziegler
Freud in 60 Minutes
ISBN 9783741227707

Walther Ziegler
Hegel in 60 Minutes
ISBN 9783741227677

Walther Ziegler
Heidegger in 60 Minutes
ISBN 9783741227752

Walther Ziegler
Kant in 60 Minutes
ISBN 9783741226373

Walther Ziegler
Marx in 60 Minutes
ISBN 9783741227691

Walther Ziegler
Nietzsche in 60 Minutes
ISBN 9783752803822

Walther Ziegler
Platon in 60 Minutes
ISBN 9783741227615

Walther Ziegler
Sartre in 60 Minutes
ISBN 9783741227653

Walther Ziegler
Rousseau in 60 Minutes
ISBN 9783741227622

Walther Ziegler
Smith in 60 Minutes
ISBN 9783741227721

Walther Ziegler
Rawls in 60 Minutes
ISBN 9783750424050

Walther Ziegler
Wittgenstein in 60 Minutes

Walther Ziegler
Adorno in 60 Minutes

Walther Ziegler
Hobbes in 60 Minutes

Walther Ziegler
Popper in 60 Minutes

Coming soon in the same series:

Walther Ziegler
Arendt in 60 Minutes

Walther Ziegler
Foucault in 60 Minutes

Walther Ziegler
Habermas in 60 Minutes

Walther Ziegler
Schopenhauer in 60 Minutes

The author:

Dr Walther Ziegler is academically trained in the fields of philosophy, history and political science. As a foreign correspondent, reporter and newsroom coordinator for the German TV station ProSieben he has produced films on every continent. His news reports have won several prizes and awards. He has also authored numerous books in the field of philosophy. His many years of experience as a journalist mean that he is able to present the complex ideas of the great philosophers in a way that is both engaging and very clear. Since 2007 he has also been active as a teacher and trainer of young TV journalists in Munich, holding the post of Academic Director at the Media Academy, an institute of higher education that offers film and TV courses at its base directly on the site of the major European film production company Bavaria Film.